PIANO • VOCAL • GUITAR

CONTEMPORARY
CHRISTIAN WEDDING
SONGBOOK

ISBN 0-7935-4291-X

HAL•LEONARD®
CORPORATION

7777 W. BLUEMOUND RD. P.O. BOX 13819 MILWAUKEE, WI 53213

PIANO • VOCAL • GUITAR

CONTEMPORARY CHRISTIAN WEDDING SONGBOOK

4 Blessing	100 Love Will Be Our Home
9 Cherish The Treasure	94 Love With Me (Melody's Song)
16 Commitment Song	112 Make Us One
28 Flesh Of My Flesh	109 O How He Loves You And Me
21 Friends For Life	118 Parent's Prayer (Let Go Of Two)
34 God Causes All Things To Grow	114 Perfect Union
39 Household Of Faith	123 Standing In The Son
42 I Call It Love	130 Sweet Adoration
64 I Love You	132 This Is The Day (A Wedding Song)
48 I Will Be Here	136 Time For Joy
54 I Will Never Go	140 To Keep Love Alive
60 In The Beauty Of Holiness	145 We Have Love
80 The Language Of Jesus Is Love	158 Wedding Prayer
86 Love	148 Where There Is Love
71 Love In Any Language	154 A Woman's Prayer (a/k/a Wedding Song)

BLESSING

Words and Music by PAM MARK HALL
and GREG LAUGHERY

With soul ♩ = 63

May God bless and al-ways keep_ you,_ wheth-er near or far_ a-way._ May you al-ways turn to Je-sus,_ with His kind and lov-ing ways. Through your_

CHERISH THE TREASURE

Words and Music by
JON MOHR

COMMITMENT SONG

Words and Music by ROBERT STERLING
and CHRIS MACHEN

FRIENDS FOR LIFE

Words and Music by MICHAEL
and STORMIE OMARTIAN

FLESH OF MY FLESH

Words and Music by
LEON PATILLO

You are flesh of my flesh, bone of my bone; there's no one clos - er. You are flesh of my flesh, bone of my bone; we are one.

GOD CAUSES ALL THINGS TO GROW

Words and Music by STEVEN CURTIS CHAPMAN
and STEVE GREEN

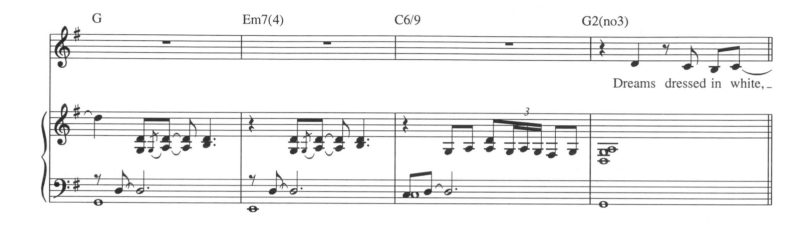

HOUSEHOLD OF FAITH

Words by BRENT LAMB
Music by JOHN ROSASCO

Here we are ___ at the start,___ com-mit-ting to ___ each
Now to be ___ a fam-i-ly ___ we've got to love ___ each

oth-er ___ by His Word and from our hearts,
oth-er at an-y cost un-self-ish-ly;

I CALL IT LOVE

Words and Music by KEITH BROWN
and BILLY SPRAGUE

Some call it old - fash-ioned now,_
Some call it fan - ta-sy,_

but I call it love._
but I call it love._

And

I WILL BE HERE

Words and Music by
STEVEN CURTIS CHAPMAN

Lyrics:
1. To-mor-row morn-in' if you___ wake up and the sun does___ not___ ap-pear,___ I,___
2. To-mor-row morn-in' if you___ wake up and the fu-ture is___ un-clear,___ I,___

I WILL NEVER GO

Words and Music by
TWILA PARIS

IN THE BEAUTY OF HOLINESS

Words and Music by
GORDON JENSON

I LOVE YOU

Words and Music by AMY GRANT
and DAN HUFF

You've got — me, I've got you,—

LOVE IN ANY LANGUAGE

Words and Music by JON MOHR
and JOHN MAYS

* - French   *** - Russian phonetic
** - Spanish   **** - Hebrew

THE LANGUAGE OF JESUS IS LOVE

Slowly, with expression

Words and Music by PHILL McHUGH, GREG NELSON,
SCOTT WESLEY BROWN and PHIL NAISH

LOVE

Words and Music by
BOB HARTMAN

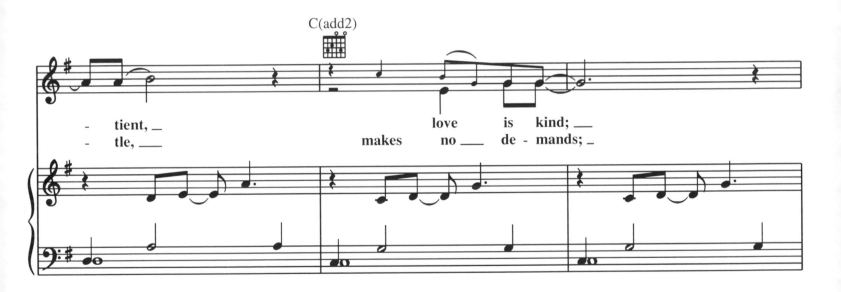

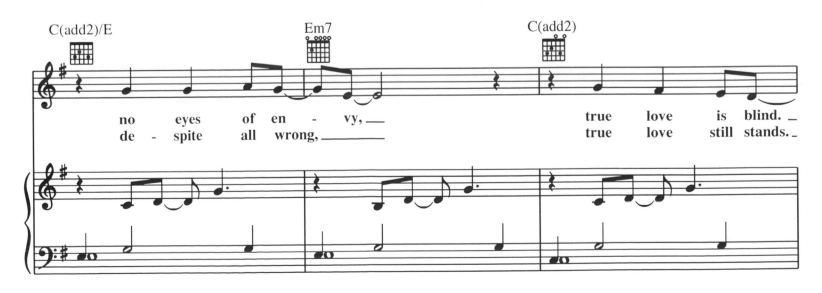

LOVE WITH ME
(MELODY'S SONG)

Words and Music by
KEITH GREEN

LOVE WILL BE OUR HOME

Words and Music by
STEVEN CURTIS CHAPMAN

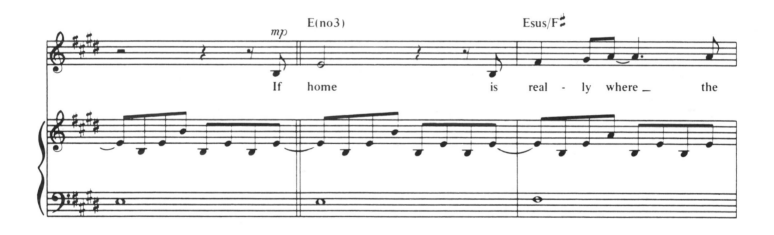

If home is real-ly where the

heart ___ is, ___ then home must ___ be a place ___

Love _____ will, love will be _ our home. _____

Love _____ will, love will be _ our home. _____

home. _____ Wher - ev - er there _ is laugh -

- ter ring - ing, _ some - one smil - ing, some - one dream - ing;

O HOW HE LOVES YOU AND ME

Words and Music by
KURT KAISER

MAKE US ONE

Words and Music by
PAUL JOHNSON

PERFECT UNION

Words and Music by JOHN ANDREW SCHREINER
and MATTHEW WARD

PARENT'S PRAYER
(LET GO OF TWO)

Words and Music by
GREG DAVIS

STANDING IN THE SON

Words and Music by PETER YORK
and RICHARD SOUTHER

Man is some - times called to live a - lone,
wom - en dream of hav - in' one to care for,

but lone - li - ness is hard for one to car -
for car - ing is a word they un - der - stand.

SWEET ADORATION

Words and Music by LYNN SUTTER ADLER,
DAWN ROGERS and BROWN BANNISTER

THIS IS THE DAY
(A WEDDING SONG)

Words and Music by
SCOTT WESLEY BROWN

Moderate double - time feeling

This is the day _____ that the Lord ___ hath ___ made, ___ And
This is the love _____ that the Lord ___ hath ___ made, ___ That

I'm so ___ glad ___ he made you.
you and ___ I ___ we are one. With

each ris - in' sun ___ you are here by my side, ___ You are
Love's mys - ter - y ___ is un - fold - ing to - day, ___

TIME FOR JOY

Words and Music by
GERRY LIMPIC

Time for joy, — **time** — **for cheer,** **that is** — **why we all** — **are here.** — **To see the un-ion of two** — **we love,** **led and** — **blessed by**

TO KEEP LOVE ALIVE

Words and Music by SCOTT DENTE,
CHRISTINE DENTE and CHARLIE PEACOCK

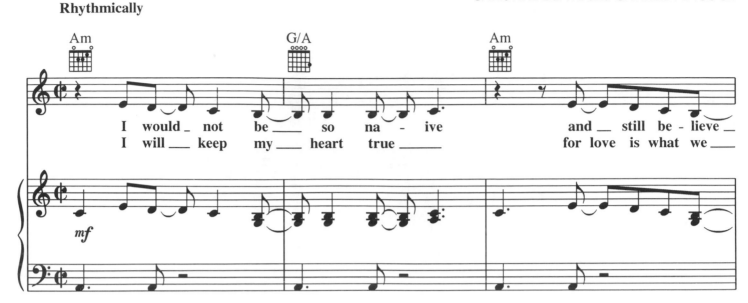

WE HAVE LOVE

Words and Music by CAROLYN HARRIS
and CHRISTOPHER KENSHAW

WHERE THERE IS LOVE

Words and Music by PHILL McHUGH
and GREG NELSON

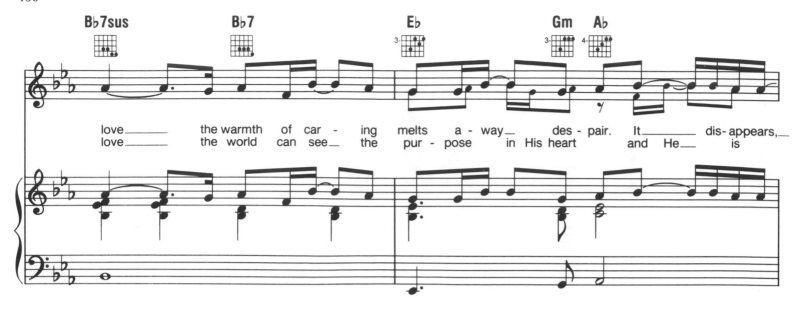

love_____ the warmth of car - ing melts a - way_ des - pair. It_____ dis- appears,_
love_____ the world can see_ the pur - pose in His heart and He_ is

known,

it_ dis - ap - pears,_ Where there is
Yes,_ He is known.

love._____

Where there is

A WOMAN'S PRAYER
(a/k/a WEDDING SONG)

Words and Music by CHRISTINE WYRTZEN
and PATRICIA FISCHER

WEDDING PRAYER

Words and Music by
MARY RICE HOPKINS